CONTENTS

Windstorm

Windstorm

Joe Denham

Nightwood Editions

Nightwood Editions
Box 1779
Gibsons, BC Canada V0N 1V0

The book has been produced on 100% post-consumer recycled, ancient-forest-free paper, processed chlorine -free and printed with vegetable-based dyes.

Cover painting by Peter Tucker: www.petertuckerdesign.com

Nightwood Editions acknowledges financial support of its publishing program from the Canada Council for the Arts and the Book Publishing Industry Development Program (BPIDP), and from the British Columbia Arts Council.

LIBRARY AND ARCHIVES CANADA CATALOGUING IN PUBLICATION

Denham, Joe, 1975–
        Windstorm / Joe Denham.

Poems.
ISBN 978-0-88971-243-0

        I. Title.

PS8557.E54W56 2009   C811'.6   C2009-903154

Printed in Canada

True singing is a different kind of breath.
A breath about nothing. A blowing in the god. A wind.

– Rainer Maria Rilke

The voices swirl down, a cyclonic cold wind
        a melody beyond the veil
they come close so I am close to hearing

as the fence binds the wood and the saw's wheel
        kicks the slab back through
my calloused fingers, which lift and feel

the searing, and the blood stream from and, true
        to gravity, down, which is
when the voices – as a flock or swarm in the blue –

swirl, wingbeats curling like oars do in water
        the air, a chorus
suddenly cued, the cries of some slaughter

with singing confused (of, say, cetaceans,
        the last of the blues,
Pacific greys homing the Bay of Conception)

the artery opened to a world now losing
        ocean life oceans wide (spirit
of its soul) and though in time life renews

it is a world beyond weeping the exiting
        blood enters, it is perpetual
shock, miasma, day upon day, it

is bees leaving the hive, then lost (little
        wonder, little wonders)
it is the cost analysis, and the cost: melting

permafrost. Perpetual shock. The centres
of gravity and buoyancy
differ: a matter of burden, ballast, and weather.

It *is* blowing in the god, this wind, without mercy.
So keeled-over I raised my blood-
soaked fingers – the voices swirling clearly

down – stretched and fisted them over wood
blown to the bone;
time spun fixed like the ripping blade as I stood

transfixed, testing the tendons, and thought, *Love
treasures hands like nothing
else*; of that point over the earth above

which no wind blows. Inside the trough
of each wave is a place
of perfect balance, where the crossing

from crest to crest calms: it is a space
time relinquishes
amidst the torrent, an interstice.

The sea. Is it remembered at all, little fish,
the stream of omphalos
blood humming, amniotic dream, wish

within the waters of a bottomless well?
The voices ring from afar
across the surface of *that* dark, like the bell

of a ship through fog, unseen. There
was no beam of light
doused upon me, nothing wavered, the air

did not alter or exalt, and I won't make shine
here what only with
great effort and good fortune occasionally glows –

it is the dime-here-dollar-there inflation, fifth-
migration money moving
in which dims, it is first class and the myth

of freedom, luxurious fiefdom, the mauve
prescription, the precipice:
each day the cumulative filicide, en masse,

our middling, meritocratic minds (mice
on an amphetamine low
lost in a lab maze while the sea ice

melts) – in our thin glass hearts, the flower
at the centre
a pressed specimen preserved post-extinction

which resonates when the voices enter
(from whichever elsewhere
we allow with whatever we measure

and weigh out this world). There is a tear
in the veil concomitant
with the flesh: the mesh of the weir-

seine we've set from the firmament
        to the low point of
the Marianas Trench torn, so filaments

slip through of the unborn-to-the-light-
        we-perceive-by, borne
on the windswept, the blinding white

voices, which wept this world to form.
        I've heard them howl
at the deck-helm of a tired hull storm-

besieged, cast wide within the full
        and open magnitude,
unmoored by any chain and anchor, soul.

The lacerations, like some forced and crude
        portal, let them sing
upstream the song which, having accrued

over time *and* space (as the dead), rang
        like the bell
of a ship through fog, unseen; the ring

clean as wind as I lifted, bucked, and fell
        (like that old hull
into the ever-rising wind-wave and swell)

not to my knees to the floor: into the squall
        of awareness: of frailty
of impermanence of the open and full

magnitude, without mercy. I manage fairly
        most days, if not to
exceed, at least to go about in an orderly

manner, managing, sadness not through
        and through, but a
manageable subtext, like the remaining blue

whales somewhere out there, ending, a
        sadness so lived with
it's underwhelming, which withers. A

felled tree, milled, always checks to the pith
        so this sadness spilled
like bound water from my centre, a tithe

to all this passing: my children born willing
        to a world diminishing
in form, diversity, beauty; our unstill

humanity overrunning – yet still the wish
        within the waters,
the seed still in those remaining, the salmon

still returning to spawn, and still the rain
        swelling the streams
to receive them, though less (both streams

and salmon, forests and seas) still the dream
        of confluence surviving
as they starve, and struggle, as ever, upstream.

This hand has sliced the flesh, reached inside
        and taken the roe
bright as sunlight, for wages. Held a hive

brittle as newly burnt ash, in first snow,
        and felt the hollow heft of
empty cells, cold as the constant wind blowing

across the decks of those fishing what's left.
        With this hand – still bleeding
as the anesthetic enters, and numbs – I'll lift

crustaceans from the sea come spring; I'll need,
        so go again to fish
down the trophic chain, turning the seeded

further to fallow. It is the line and hook
        we cast *and* swallow,
the surface float of the spirit; the sinker.

The doctor pierced his thread and needle
        deep into my finger,
brought it up and cinched the ragged wound

shut, the small wound, which would linger
        but heal over, becoming
in time only another scar-line, tiny reminder

to keep mindful in the midst of the coming
        storm. We are born
naked and warm and without blame; come

blind and unbreathing into the light, scorn
        and sadness surrounding
and love, swirling like the voices borne

from elsewhere (a high wind from offshore).
        I watched an old man
wander the ER, his chest bare, the sound

from within like the rattle of uplift on cheap tin
        roofing, the whole house
(his aged body) shuddering in the gusts. I can

almost forgive his fragility, though the use
        is only to forgive
my own: stone within stone: a home

a happiness, in light of and even so, living
        well with no-hope (that empty
moniker of the mind) as though the heart could give

over so easily to what's inevitable. The sea-
        green curtain was drawn
and he was gone, my ear suddenly vacant

of his breath, and the voices too passed beyond
        my hearing, or I receded
from them, the wound sutured, the rough-sawn

splinters flushed, the adrenaline rush subsided
        and the surgical lamp
turned down, my blood wiped and washed away.

In the silence I become a sieve the limitless stars
        and sand grains and working
working hands wash through; in the vacuum-shine

my dull and limited mind, in its shadow-thinking
        the big bang post-nothing
which is the emperor's unclothing (is not nothing

itself a vast unending something?); sinking
        under that free-water
weight shifting the point of lever linking

gravity's and buoyancy's centres, in wonder
        well-sprung, I'll swim:
where to begin, without ending? We're asunder

and put so at the source: the thin and naked skin,
        the night-blind vision
and the fear that keeps us gathered within

the circumference of our ceaseless fires; a scion
        overgrown, its wide shadow
denying photosynthesis to its withered origin.

The two-by-twelve fir that razored through
        my fingers was milled
from a thousand-year-old tree that fell low

in a wind that built itself steady (a huge swell
        surging through wide oceans
of air) gale- to storm- to hurricane-force filling

the sail of branches atop that statuary soul –
　　　　　master of what, in one
place, is attainable – till its platform root

lay vertical, and I took shelter from the sun
　　　　　in the dark fecund
soil newly born to light, each tendril-umbilicus

drying out in summer's scorch. *Torch the fund*
　　　　　managers' bank books
and balance sheets, I was thinking. *End*

wealth's glittering negation of beauty. The hook
　　　　　and line we both cast
and swallow. The voices sang there in the crook

of god's arm: untoiled ground – some of the last –
　　　　　the sound faint as a light
wind through the high trees still standing. Then nothing.

The voices are always there. It is their old, sweet
　　　　　song keeps this world,
though we hear them only as a child in the night

hearing for the first time through the fold
　　　　　of sleep the song
of whales surfacing dark water, the purled

and perfect water opening over and along
　　　　　their ancient bodies. I hold
the doctor's pale hand, the curtain now drawn

open and the light again upon my skin. What's sold
                and bought but tiny fragments
of soul? The hands with kindness or malice or cold

anger constructing and harvesting the fulfillment
                of what we've thus far
mined and imagined; with love or resentment

each thing circulating, hand to hand, our
                selves sifted out from
their sequestered cores: this currency: hour

upon hour, the windstorm which gathers, will come.
                He isolates each joint
and I grip and resist. Every trauma leaves a sun-

spot on the brain, its size in proportion to the point
                of impact and its residual
impact through time, so the mind's flow forever eddies

there where the voices crossed over, contrapuntal
                to our dissonant array.
We live in the accrual, this beautiful madrigal.

He places gauze over the scattering of stitches, my flayed
                flesh rejoined, the gales
of pain gusting again from fingertip to brain. I prayed

as I drove the long road to the hospital, to this god
                we're within, for mercy,
a wound that would heal. He offered his hand as I stood.

You know son, he said. *You're a very lucky man.*

(The Abandoned Orchard)

to be possessed or
abandoned by a god
is not in the language

– John Thompson

No one remembers which great wind it was
laid these old trees down as though dreaming
leaf bud flower fruit. Autumn sun streams
like smoke through amber leaves, live fire's
sister: green flaring to gold to the cold
broken ground – trees spilling to sky
from earthen gourds their roots bore
to water before wind tore them over.
                              Old
sweet song, none of us sings with you sweetly –
if ever we did – any longer.
No one remembers, nor
                    hears clearly inside the sweep
of electromagnetic signals (desire's
echoes)
          though we reach through those immaterial wires

to take the last of the fruit this fallen orchard sings forth.

All night the roof sounds the onslaught
of wind-driven rain. East, and near, another fir
breaks free its mooring so morning occurs
uncoiled – an unbound knot.
                                        Stillness.
Apparent now in wind's recession
as silence following a low plane's passing;
the abundance of the past
          amidst present depletion.

Nightlong, I woke to wall-shaking gusts
from the dream of dark water flooding
the aft deck; the dream of water frozen

beyond land flooded with dust.

Wind of the mind:
                              windswell of blood:

the same on deck as the cold water rose
as on the dry shore, scanning the floes.

The obvious allusion, the myth of
the garden – old fiction: archaic
delusion – casts its insistent, stoic
pall over the poem, the way dove
connotes peace, and war, which in turn
calls up Dostoevsky, grey light, oil.
The seaweed we gather to feed the soil
heaps in on November's first churning
gale-storm, rich with the dying alkaline.
While we shovel and haul, carrion crows
clear the estuary of spawned-out coho
scattering the flats. Not Hopkins'. Not mine.
But the world's, in and of (as we are, as song)
the unattainable wind, arriving and gone.

The boat burns in the windless night, its fire's
dark light threading in from the middle distance
over waveless water, black and slick
as tarmac after rain. The endless wick
of the city mauves the underbelly
of sky beyond, the boat burning slowly
northward on the flood, smoke rust and bruise-
black billowing off the flames.
                              Forced to choose
I'd torch it down and take the money too.
One too many seasons in the secession
of seasons siphoning off the last life-
blood of a sea sick with eutrophication
till its death and the debt hone a knife
on the wind, course with self-scorn and blame –
the match struck and set, I'd swim from the flame.

I could list the ocean's full anamnesis
(simile: image: as patient, supine);
which of us doesn't want the coniine
the cross the irrefutable thesis

to stand, die behind. Though few give
their lives, life's work, much less their
shipped, shellacked apples, their hot air
dryers.
      I'd say what it means to live
with no-hope (and how) if I didn't know
you were listening only with your own
voice anyhow.
          As it is, I've sewn
torn, re-sewn: nothing saved; nothing slows

the die-off (x number of species per hour)
to what will be left; will be ours.

Unseasonable snows blanket the windfalls
the branches, the timbers that once were
joist, beam and strapping here.
                              Sappho's
sweetapple, efflorescent in the unexpected
the unaccustomed white, perches bird-
like in song, as sunrays cloud-split; word
as though word were reborn, resurrected.

The weave – what's connected unequivocally
– unequivocally unraveling
                              on arctic outflows;
the disparity of what was given and what we chose.

And choose:
                    I'll climb the ashen limbs
above this abandoned roofline as the west sky dims,
take that sweetness in as the autumn
                              and dusk transpose.

There was a time then it passed, the body.
Machinery now, its corollaries (land
gone passé, as silence, and stars): grand-
father on warfarin and Eprex at ninety.
The few hours, you wouldn't know his spirit
from '83, though about him, in the air
a presence, a pre-sense of the bare
hour, the long tunnel (it's said) lit
like sunlight through the surface of the sea.

This hull holds the ocean not unlike a soul
holds the air for a moment as it pulls
then drifts away. Which may or may not be
god's machinery, or fear; an elsewhere
that intimates but won't cohere.

In the clear morning calm, in the quiet
fear, the first whisper of what blood-
light piercing grey cloud presages
in the charged air: the wire filament
surging spine, the sense: as the cold moon
siphons the tide, inside, beyond the cage
reason rages against receiving, this world.

I swear I collapsed on the float and unfurled
like a flag in the fast-rising wind. And lay,
bare as beach-washed bone, in the fray
we've sewn, torn, and re-sewn…
then rose, and turned my heart toward home:
your heart: from the gathering storm. Where
to begin, without ending, love? I love you. There.

My saw then silent the clearing reclaimed
the quiet it was as forest before I came,
engine in hand, orchard and house-site

in mind. Birdsong and a warm June rain
fell from and upon trees still standing
and for a time – a blue heron landing

atop the high fir over the iron pin –
I felt as I had as a child, before this
question of whether even to try is *ignis*

fatuus, when living and being in
the world simply was, not an idea
to be written of and discussed. Off the sea

a gust washed over broad maples, slanting rain,
and I set down to file the chain.

It is the world beyond weeping you walk through
its doors its wide fields with fading light

beneath the charred pines the delicate blue
veins, the diagnoses, the blinding white

machines. Having learnt, finally, to forgive?
This goddamn dissentious blood. This brain:

all of life's living just learning to live:
when water falling finally sounds it's no longer rain.

In time there will be pain and it will be
all I can do to rise and let the wind

through an open window, the distant sea
singing you through. Each night, each end

brings what binds us: our love, and fear.
It is enough, each day, to have been here.

Entwining the airwaves with which our odium
is cast as a net over the Earth, broadcast
to and through the plenum – erasure of the last
silence, the wisdom – sings the sea's requiem

in the windsong. This is no translation,
this long-line tow trawling the abyssal
silt, oceanic-soul, in the low opaline
light sifting down through fire's alburnum.

I stood on the aft deck watching the day's
catch weaken to waste under harsh fluorescents
in a dark wind, coming to the cold essence
as the storm swarmed down into the bay.

And wondered why I had ever sung, or how,
of this sea fished to fallow; the sky's lachrymal.

The arbutus articulate the form, the anorexic myelin the wind-
worn autonomic: each burl, trough and bend borne
in on wave-backs built
                        and broken on the storm-
wheel, cast and set in greenwood madrone –

blackened, blight-stricken branches susurrate
the foothills of storm the way the strait
carries orca exhales opening
                        night like wind.
Beyond the grove
        the island's igneous
                slides wave- and wind-

shorn to water: the mind finds a home in the exposure
        and feeds like fire on air:

the eye in the storm of desire: despair; the sky
        and its clouds, descending, belie

the presence: (wind's massive, moulding hand) the field
fluctuant, ever-emergent, to which we yield.

It wakes me in the dark this knowing
      they should not have left and will not
return.
      The calyx burn, the high and unharvested, the rotten
balsam planks and nails rusting back to mineral dust. The flowing

fires. No one remembers where to or why: in the whorl
and coil, the wind-fuelled, the raging, who cares?
                                         It flares
and our feet alight, thrusting us forward through the forward-facing world

we've built within this world which won't sleep.
                                  I climb the steep
incline of the sweep
                the fallen trees have taken

back towards the sun, and arrive in myself awakened

to the windows humming in the wind; the bright unseen
trill of songbirds in the attic
                   falling through the dark as of a dream.

As where a wind blows.
I can teach you that.
The form of despair we call "the world."

– Jorie Graham

The fencelines' bow in lateral profile,
      the bent stalks broken I walk out
and over into the field, the wind so still sunlight

is silence spread through upswirling seed. The sea
      frightens, and so keeps me
inconsequential: it's too simple to see this

as aftermath, as though wind were not endless
      and so endlessly singing
despite cities: our sickness: the wars.

When last inside the cyclogenesis I stood aside
      the freeway, upon affluvial earth,
the river's estuary receiving the floodtide behind me

and watched cars careen those they carry
      through habitat turned farmland turned finally
to thoroughfare for the speed we've acquired,

and understood in that place beyond the tail-chasing mind
      where truth settles like silt in time's
accumulation, compression, that it's not a question

of rethinking the grid, or god,
      or the flower at the centre of our thin glass hearts,
which are broken. It was never tears the ocean

required, but with our metaphors hardwired to language's
      dwindling source
we wept, we weep, and our weeping

has been, and is, for us alone. The world being
a world away. I walk within
myself within the field, within the near-stillness

of wind's recession, amidst the scattered seed cones
over the bent stalks
the saturated soil, with self-derision, without

hope. There is a long rope I reach for
to lift past the abaude, each reluctant morning,
its frayed end-knot just within grasp.

I clasp tightly while moment to moment the world
diminishes, our children's unwitting
laughter ringing from their room beyond the wall.

There's another squall in the far-off approaching,
its deep grey delineating
the distance. The hands that weave the rope are

resistance; the strands, the substance, are love.
There is an altitude above
which no wind blows. I am standing

at sea level in the first swirlings of storm
listening for the song
like an animal quickened in the imminence

feeling the finite potential, the hard limits
of the senses like a cage
door closing. I know the flickering felt

is said to be ions colliding. What's underlying
        can't yet be spoken of.
That it may have something to do with love

requires faith, in this world beyond weeping,
        a tear. The sky is clear
to the stormline, deep blue deepening over the sea

as it breathes forth the world from its depths.
        Everyone knows something
crept from some littoral mudflat as it was once

understood we were moulded on the sixth day
        from dust. The Earth's crust
floats on an ocean of magma as the orb

hurtles through space. There is a veil
        thin as shadow
thin as sunlight sifting through upswirling

seed. Wind's weave. I imagine
        when I leave
I'll climb hand over hand the rope

I cling fast to, knowing nothing
        of where it leads,
nothing of what might anchor it there from where

it falls. But even that fails. Which takes the wind
        from the proverbial
sails, no? or leaves them hanging

half-hoisted, wind riffling clear through.
        Dark grey swallows the blue
like wildfire would this field, the storm seething

stronger as it swarms. I remember hauling
        south of Black Point,
a massive cloudbank soaring up the strait.

They say a seaman's only a seaman once
        he's watched the sea
seal over the final few inches of his

ship's sinking stern. Which was my fear
        as the under-
estimated wind slammed in, water

heaping over the bulwarks and fire-
        hosing through
the scuppers. It's the sentiment that un-

steadies me now, knowing vulnerability
        is never fully felt
until the hull is sucked forever under.

It's a wonder, each day, what remains
        still enlivened
despite the decline; what retains god's

vigour, its flickering fire. That we're here
        in this field
I conjure though the real

waters rise and winds collide
       with what's left
to work with and for: the world

like a cage door closing, the aperture
       lapsing as the storm
dilates, despair within dichotomy

interwoven: of us inspun, uplifting
       on the mezzo cyclone,
Earth stripped bare as unburied bone.

Our only home. I recall as a small child
       thinking Earth's axis
was a steel rod upon which it spun,

skewered, through night and day.
       Not knowing then
how the shadow is cast we live

half our lives in, darkened –
       I'll set us down now
low in the grass, so the wind will flow over

light as glass, the remnant blue
       drifting to grey
as the squall rains down on the field

and us here, incidental in the howling
       plenitude,
lifting with its rise even as it falls.

It is how I know the rope is made for winding around and around the wind.

– Amy Bespflug

South of Black Point, southeast wind screaming
the shadow of death in my eyes, seven days into storm
since the sea lay down calm as my son does now sleeping
calm and distant as the milk-white moon, as the milk
of our mothers we remember only as memory
more distant than stars;
                              memory we tie fast to
as mooring, unmoored, adrift without instrument inside the open blue
to the endless; or ending; or unknown shore.

We exited the mouth as day came – dim-lit, diffuse –
darkly through wind-riven, low flying cloud,
leaden-centred like the line we'd soon haul.
From inlet-calm to swell so fierce it was wanting-
mommy-like-a-baby fear.
                              Not a moment for a
thought of the clear-as-glass sea we'd worked before the storm,
everything inside chaos being kinesthetic
                              being
reaction upon reaction being accumulation being a function

of the wind that builds the waves that wash always over the working-
one-season-from-poor:
                              no door to close against the rising wind
no shelter between storm and skin.

We hauled fast our gear from the abyssal sea floor, each trap run through
        like a rung on a ladder a frightened miner
                climbs from the catacomb of a collapsing
mineshaft. Frantic. Seven days in the ripstream, our adrenaline-mend
on exhaustion fraying
                        at the seam. Still the traps sprung

through walls of water, from the sucking striated troughs
    they spun, and slammed the bulwarks, the mast
        tugging its turnbuckles and bolts with every
pitch from starboard to port, swaying like the sail of branches atop
that old fir before it thundered down.

    Standing in the shadow
of its vertical platform-root – each tendril
umbilicus drying out in summer's scorch – is entering

a clearing of pure yin: deep, deep feminine. It settles
the nerve-worn spirit. Cools the liver's smouldering wind-
burn fire, kidneys milking the soul up from dark
ground newly born to light, fecund soil

that sustained the tree century upon century before
winter brought a deluge, rotting its root-grip,
and gale- swelled to storm- swelled to hurricane-
force strong, a steady soaring surge which tore
that statuary soul from its breathing inside
the wide ocean of air.
        We knew we were caught there,
wind shredding waves to tornadoes of mist
like translucent angels straining free of the ether,
ephemeral, whipped back on their tethers; the sea
a stadium of fury, a field of wind-fired effigy,

our lives' likenesses ten thousand times over, stoking in the squall.

Taoists believe persistent wind will blow down
deep in the self, swirling a torrent of madness or twisting
the bodymind to a slight, static posture off-kilter the way
branches grow one-sided from straight trunks.
                                        Late winter,
in the midst of that gale-scattered grey, I climb out
to Poor Man's Rock (stunted trees streaming in stasis
like seized weathervanes) and thrust my bare face
seaward, windward, into the thread-thin exposure
a decade at sea builds need for
like fire's for air.
                    The wind's frigid flame
scorching back my cloistered spirit
to bare land, broken and ready.

Nothing or everything prepares one for the flood-
tide to turn and ebb against the ever-rising
wind.
        The swells – almost lulling all morning, steady
as a hypnotist's stare – heaved, shifting from rollers to
walls of white-streaked grey, as though the sea had gone
schizophrenic, each curl of water split by the bow
a cry (as of the sea's own sorrow): screaming
the shadow of our hostility, which we tally
but never see clearly, the way my son sees
his reflection in still water, yet still
misunderstands what it is looking back.

What history tells us is what we were
on that boat was a scale model for
the frantic world, warring and loving and open
to whatever the elements and random events might
make of our lives warring and loving and open
for business, which is what, ultimately, we were
doing out there, hauling gear amidst wind-hell for
wages, with war over the horizon and nothing in sight
but interest due for taxes unpaid and interest due for
the house the boat the dime-here-dollar-there
inflation that leaves you wishing loving were
more simple, a light wind through an open
window, the salt air and the distant height
of Mt. Arrowsmith in the blue afternoon… remember?

Love forms its own weather. Currents of air
colliding in time, contingent, metaphor upon
metaphor, but still the hard matter of fight
upon fight between feedings and sleep and hour
after hour of the hauler, or computer, or whatever
work we set all else aside for…

A white curtain drawn by a whisper of air.
Fresh-milled fir reddening in late-August light.
Warm rain beyond the window left open
onto the land we care and toil for,
our newborn son sleeping peacefully there.

Something was broken, something integral to the system was
dysfunctioning so the water froze and thawed, freezing and
warming while the fish suffered

                          in the fluctuation, suffocating.
Under a clusterfuck of stars (the names of which I've never
cared to learn, knowing beauty sometimes
most in the exogenous unminded, thus unmarred)

           a coked-up refer-man pissed at being
called late in the off-hours barked inane unreasoning over
a cell signal lightly radiating my brain from one of the swarm
of satellites circling the Earth, the worth of piscine life less
to him than an eightball in his little dark mess of an existence.

Persistent endogenous sickness.

Alone, I threw the phone against the wheelhouse wall
and wailed disvotive hatred from the stern into
the nightscape, worn by the week of twenty-hour
days in rough wind, engines roaring endlessly underfoot.

I shut them down, switched the deck lights off, and stood
in the chime of that darkness, trying to breathe and bring
myself back.
           Later I tossed the dead fish overboard
into phosphorescent water, one after the other lit
for a time and falling fast and bright as stars.

We were working one season from, one sinking
from, one wrist strangled
                            and severed by the setting
line, one market decline, one algae over-
                    bloom from, one backroom
department decree, one pinhole in the waterline,
                one slip over the gunwale making a pine box of the sea.

That far from, and that near to, freedom. One
                weakness or erosion in our link
of instinct
to the storm's mind
                    which could give

and set the point of gravity sliding toward the point of buoyancy till the point

is reached beyond which the hull
                                shudders, and will not right,
wall upon wall of white
                    galloping, wind-spurned water

pounding the freeboard over, then under. We were in the ricochet
        the reverberation
                            thunder hammering down the northern slopes
thunder's echo over our meager

our measly efforts, our affront in the face

                of the gods we were damned *and* driven by: the clear light
fear throws through the eye
                    and the gaping chakras
sucking the sky

    clean as the polished shards
cobbling our hearts into some splintered semblance of wholeness.

The flower at the centre gone
    to seed, to wind like a weed that won't

let up invading the designated floralry, design greenery, the facade
    fronting the consensus factory bureaucracy

till the well-to-do are whipped to a tizzy
    confounded by the failure of their chemical
 oligarchy.

The sea inside the sea seemed to rise
    with the wind's levity (we were *so*
       small, after all) which was not without
mercy, though it is only
    looking back as I do now that allows

me to assign the wind leniency
    which is all too human a
  quality, and rings
false
  as the *god* leitmotif in this poem, ultimately.

But wind the world over needs ten thousand names
  and storm and song ten thousand more
and so our subsequent poverty, our stifled ontology

leaves a chasm between Camus' trinity
    and the tiny inklings of otherness, of elsewhere often
  glimpsed but always utterly ungrasped.

Ground ungained. If I feign certainty it's always only to draw
a curtain across the pane that quivers in the winnowing wind.
It is the fear of finding a life threshed more of chafe than grain.
Arms outstretched, hands upturned, walking on water, holding
up the sky. (If I were wholly vetted of delusion I wouldn't be
cloistered here in the early hours composing, as you wouldn't
be here searching for something to inscape. Similarly afflicted.
Symbiotically affected. Though the effect I have on you, and you
on I, is our collective collusion: the con of each singular self, or
selves in concert, holding up the sky, which is falling.)

The storm broke as the sun cut an amber seam between the dark
clouds and darker horizon. The flowing fire falling. The feral
wind recoiling. And the adrenal flood draining back so a small
precipice for thought came clear. In this world beyond weeping,
a tear.

And I saw then how we'd been working as close to god – if god
be the sum of the world's elements which collide and combine to
build storm: if storm be everything temporal fully overcome by
that energy elemental – as close to god as a woman bearing down
in the throes of birth. And the earth we worked, flooded under one
hundred fathoms of water – earth that once was molten and will be
mountain slope – and the rope we haul and the one we've held
which we've spliced and woven around each other. The ship *and*
the anchor. Love chosen, each day, despite the many winds which
rack its walls, which weather its hull and rigging.

(In this memory there is always singing, so faint, the melody more
distant than what's seen – song in sepia – like full sunlight from its
centrifugal source just breaking through, the cloudbanks' grey
undermined by rainlight shine's array.)

Everything in the wrong wind
will waver. Everything eventually falls. The squalls
kept coming, cumulative chaos, and the wonder that we're here

to recall, to sift back
                    to that maelstrom

is the sheer racket of chance. Circumstance upon circumstance
            into the random stitchings and siphonings
of time compounded we call *a life*. Cipher of the end

and the beginning like a thought
                                        balloon burst. There is no
                        forward trajectory no
blossoming humanity
                        blessed.

            Your best guess is as good and ridiculous
as the next,
                as far as god goes. We're all in the throes.

Regardless, wind blows slantwise, straight-on, sidereal, singing through
            our thin-as-smoke skin.
                                We hauled the last
trap of the day and ran for harbour, slackening seas
                heaving the stern-
quarter to near
                instability as you spooled the last string out
like a spider's swaddling silk:
                                alone at your work,
one slip from the cold sea,
                    the impossibility of recovery

from the still-steep-swell: one slip
                              from eternity (whatever
        that may or may not be)

the certainty of the nothing
                    of your absence here

haunting me as I worked the helm to hold the set's edge

as it does now knowing
                    I would wander

adrift without instrument inside the open blue
        through this world beyond

keeping, mute and screaming, the shadow of death in my eyes.

Therefore does the wind keep blowing
that holds this great Earth in the air.

– Jack Gilbert

(Nothing found) sound within sound: blowing wind inside
the spiracle exhale of whales surfacing black water; flaring gusts
of fire in water's break and backslide against the shore; beyond
this: relative silence, unceasing whir of matter spinning
under range:
                    the strange, insistent sense
of connection, near-comprehension: the old, sweet song
nearly not unheard.

The one word (it's said) which won't be spoken.

The token attempt. The territory flagged and mapped
terraced and tilled
                      filled with wire and wheel and steel-
studded concrete
                      structures scraping the sky. The eye
of the storm: (silence stillborn) the *I*-insectine

fretting the *mu*-points
                      the gridlines the further

reaches, the last breeding beaches and the far
                far north, where so much will be asked of.

As though this or any other, any other's
　　　lucubration could capture the imagination
as though some imagination might somehow
　　　in the imagining solve for x
as though some x or other were what's needed to be
　　　solved for or sought
as though in seeking there might be finally found or thought...

(The sound the wind makes moving through each hole
inside the particles composing *you* is the chime
of time filling god's iron begging bowl slowly
emptying the body of the soul sensed as *I*.)

Given to violence. (Which was and is
                                    one of many means
of existence.) The winds we respire rise and rive, and rivet
other species to reduction. Given *that* predilection
wherein lies hope?
                        Braiding and unbraiding and
braiding the rope.
                       I remember forgetting
the warnings as the dopplering drone descended and
the planes passed low
                       through the blue
pre-dawn darkness overhead, dropping their chemical
cargo over miles of forest and waking houses.

And still I walked out to meet the day's first light
speckling down as that spray-mist landed.

What when what was
polyphonic begins to drone and the latest
führer becomes fodder for offhand humour—

what when famine becomes funny?

When we've morphed so far (which moult?
which instar?) we cower (it may be

no one survives the city, the sonic
                              saturation, with dignity:

it's unrelenting, its unrelinquishing suction:
the wholesale sell-off, the hinterland absorption).

Souls spun in swaddling silk. Sucklings. That ilk.

As though like a sky it might come clear inside
the body windy with inevitability; this world
fully bio- and geo-engineered (a set shield of up-
spun particles levitating over the poles precisely
at that height in the thermosphere where
no wind nor breath blows).
                              While there are those
millions living where the floes' meltwater
will flood;
              those living as though already forgiven
for the risen seas acidly burned barren as
though there were some god or prophet given
to grant what is only for those
innocents gone or yet to come to give.

                    (There is no language
for what it will mean to live once the final pelagic spawn
sifts down to the depths, dead as stone;
              no name for those still living as though there will be and is
nothing for which to atone.)

Then the wind-spurned recusancy eases to
a light, benevolent anarchy and art
                            to cautious redaction

(the much considered antecedents answered) and the sun comes

cupreous and inculpable through the clouds
                            and we are
      carried forth to the expectantly
                            cadenced conclusion.

Our collective collusion. It is the old song
                            recycled and rescored
in discord with the writhings and ragings
unceasing;
            the exponential toxins
accumulating in the biosphere and our catalytic, sequestered fear.

(The one unaltered melody
                    inaudible above the rising and sheer.)

Because my daughter says, "Geesh!" and struggles to stand
one hand gripping the coffee table one hand waving
in elation
              I rise too, each day trying still
to learn the language, the small steps sturdily taken.

Awaken with the ghost of elsewhere or the random
firings of my mind's nocturnal repairings
and turn again to the workaday, and the greater work

to be done (the one god: the sun; and the other
like a shadow over every shoulder:
                                  the endless, and ending:
the unknown shore).
                     Her animate joy like a spore in the air

seeding the ground *our* struggles form and furrow
that it may someday spring and sing forth –

(A song of carbonic acid scouring the oceans;
        of salps swarming the otherwise
empty?)

        The seven seas nodding on their stalks
while our clocks count our minutes
and hours and years.

(A song of fears of failures of narrowing measures.)

Are these the narrating lines, fines
        sifting from coarser aggregates, the necessary
                                    convulsions?

A song of long forgone conclusions: (Of love that wasn't

clearly after all
                all of what was required.)

The stories come to us like the light of stars
long past, supernovae older than the Earth.

How can you reprove words, Job asks,
when the speech of a despairing man is wind?

Where then to begin? Begin at the beginning,
then begin: consider chemosynthesis, the filament

of matter which may be
                                    unity in a unified theory:

the possibility of infinite possibility. Yet still the seas
so swiftly ending, by our hands, and the sickly water

I feed my son and daughter worsening daily as does
all that's left of this world with which they must learn

now to make do (sadness, through and through) adrift
as they are, as we are, without bearing, without ballast,

inside this windstorm obscuring, and the ocean-blue…

The Rilke lines are from *Duino Elegies*; the translation is by Galway Kinnell and Hannah Liebmann.

"Love treasures hands like nothing else" is from John Berger's novel *Lilac and Flag.*

"the stream of omphalos blood humming" is Galway Kinnell's phrase from his poem "Under the Maud Moon."

"masters of what, in one place, is attainable" is John Pass's phrase from his poem "Invocation to the Character of Water."

The John Thompson lines are from his poem "Apple Tree."

"Sappho's sweetapple" refers to Anne Carson's translation of Fragment 105a.

The Jorie Graham lines are from her poem "The Guardian Angel of Not Feeling."

The Amy Bespflug lines are from her poem "The Reasons I've Been Silent."

The Jack Gilbert lines are from his poem "Adulterated."

"the seas nodding on their stalks" is W.S. Merwin's phrase from his poem "For a Coming Extinction."

The verse from the Book of Job is 6:26.

ACKNOWLEDGMENTS

The first five pages of *Windstorm* were previously published in *Lake: A Journal of Arts and Environment.*

"No one remembers which great wind it was" was previously published as *Abandoned Orchard* alongside John Thompson's *Apple Tree* as part of High Ground Press' *Companions Series* limited edition broadsides.

Thank you to the editors of each, and to Pete, and to Silas and everyone at Nightwood.

Thank you to the Canada Council for the Arts for financial support.

This book is to and for B.

KEITH SHAW

Joe Denham's first collection, *Flux*, was published in 2003. His work has appeared in numerous magazines and anthologies including *Open Field*, *The New Canon*, *Breathing Fire 2*, *Jailbreaks*, and *In Fine Form*. He lives with his family in Halfmoon Bay, BC, where he works as a fisherman and a traditional timber framer.